D1519652

LEATHERFACE

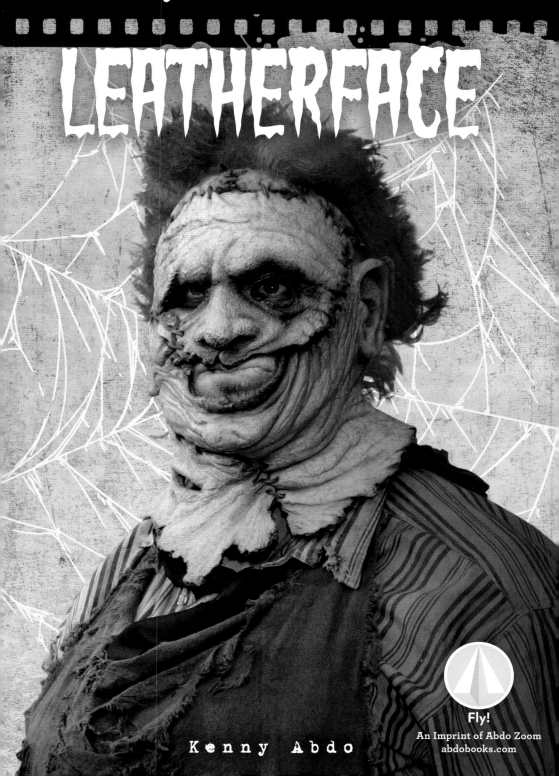

Kenny Abdo

Fly!
An Imprint of Abdo Zoom
abdobooks.com

abdobooks.com

Published by Abdo Zoom, a division of ABDO, P.O. Box 398166, Minneapolis, Minnesota 55439. Copyright © 2020 by Abdo Consulting Group, Inc. International copyrights reserved in all countries. No part of this book may be reproduced in any form without written permission from the publisher. Fly!™ is a trademark and logo of Abdo Zoom.

Printed in the United States of America, North Mankato, Minnesota.
052019
092019

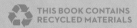

THIS BOOK CONTAINS
RECYCLED MATERIALS

Photo Credits: Alamy, AP Images, Everett Collection, Getty Images, Shutterstock
Production Contributors: Kenny Abdo, Jennie Forsberg, Grace Hansen
Design Contributors: Dorothy Toth, Neil Klinepier

Library of Congress Control Number: 2018963568

Publisher's Cataloging-in-Publication Data

Names: Abdo, Kenny, author.
Title: Leatherface / by Kenny Abdo.
Description: Minneapolis, Minnesota : Abdo Zoom, 2020 | Series: Hollywood
    monsters set 2 | Includes online resources and index.
Identifiers: ISBN 9781532127472 (lib. bdg.) | ISBN 9781532128455 (ebook) |
    ISBN 9781532128943 (Read-to-me ebook)
Subjects: LCSH: Texas chain saw massacre (Motion picture)--Juvenile literature. |
    Leatherface (Motion picture : 1974)--Juvenile literature. | Horror films--
    Juvenile literature. | Motion picture characters--Juvenile literature.
Classification: DDC 791.43616--dc23

TABLE OF CONTENTS

LEATHERFACE

The 1974 film, *The Texas Chain Saw Massacre,* is about a group of friends traveling through Texas. When their van runs out of gas they meet Leatherface and his **cannibalistic** family.

5

The Texas Chain Saw Massacre is considered one of the most influential horror movies in cinema history. That wouldn't be possible without its leading monster, Leatherface.

ORIGIN

Director and co-writer Tobe Hooper got the idea for the film while holiday shopping. He was very frustrated with the crazy crowds. Hooper found himself in the chain saw aisle. He thought, "I know a way to get through this crowd really quickly."

9

With the crazy concept down, Hooper also wanted the film to reflect the time he was living in. The lies the US government told the people in relation to the **Vietnam War** and the **Watergate** scandal inspired him.

Hooper based Leatherface partly on real-life killer Ed Gein. He felt that "the real monster was man, not fantasy."

HOLLYWOOD

The film was shot on location in Texas. The crew worked during a brutal heat wave. Temperatures reached more than 100°F (37.7°C) every day!

Hooper cast mostly unknown actors from Texas. That way it would be more authentic. Gunnar Hansen played the hulking mute, Leatherface.

Leatherface wears three different masks throughout the movie. Hansen imagined the killer he played having no personality or human qualities beneath the mask.

Hooper falsely marketed his movie
as a true story. The buzz worked.
Droves of horror fans flocked to the
theaters. The low-budget film was a
huge hit!

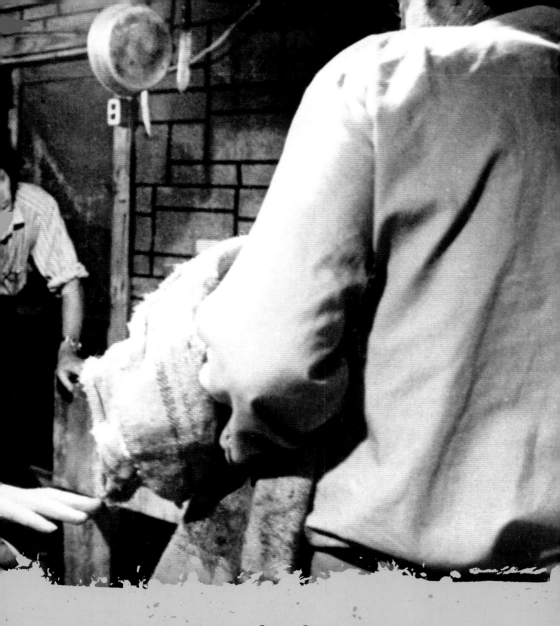

However, it proved to be too scary for some viewers. People walked out of screenings horrified. The film was banned in many countries.

LEGACY

Despite its reputation as a gruesome film, there is little gore and on-screen violence. The filmmakers actually set out for a PG rating.

19

Several **sequels**, **prequels**, and **reboots** have been made. In all, seven actors have put on the mask and picked up the chain saw.

IN 1974, ONE MOVIE CHANGED THE FACE OF HORROR.
IN 2013, A DARK NEW CHAPTER BEGINS.

TEXAS
CHAINSAW 3D

EVIL WEARS MANY FACES

Production company Legendary Pictures bought the **rights** to *The Texas Chain Saw Massacre* in 2018. They are planning to make a new movie and TV series.

GLOSSARY

cannibalism – eating your own kind.

prequel – a movie, or other work that includes earlier events from an existing story.

reboot – a new start to a movie franchise, recreating plots, characters, and backstory.

rights – legally owning a movie property.

screening – the showing of a film in a movie theater.

sequel – a movie, or other work that continues the story begun in a preceding one.

Vietnam War – a war between South Vietnam and North Vietnam from 1957 to 1975. The United States was also involved.

Watergate – a political scandal involving President Richard Nixon in 1972. As a result, many people went to jail and Nixon resigned in 1974.

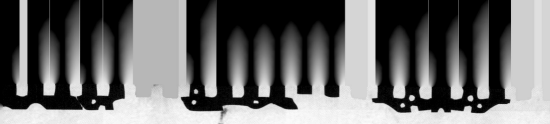

ONLINE RESOURCES

To learn more about Leatherface, please visit abdobooklinks.com or scan this QR code. These links are routinely monitored and updated to provide the most current information available.

INDEX